Beadwork Treasures
The Designs of
Gillian Lamb

First published 2007

© Gillian Lamb

Published by Word4Word, Evesham, UK
www.w4wdp.com

The right of Gillian Lamb to be identified as
Author of this work has been asserted by her in
accordance with the Copyright, Design & Patents
Act 1988.

ISBN-10 0-9551677-6-0
ISBN-13 978-0-9551677-6-8

A CIP catalogue record of this book is available
from the British Library.

Printed in the UK by Cromwell Press.

Contents

About the Author

Gillian Lamb is a seasoned knitter who fell in love with beading in 1998 after working with patterning software. She has taught extensively in the United Kingdom and the United States. She also taught at the first Bead Art Show in Kobe, Japan in October 2006. Gillian likes to take a different perspective to her beading, looking at colour and texture as she works. Her work has also been published in many books.

Gillian has been very active in the Beadworkers Guild and in 2001 won the Guild's annual challenge.

She lives in Surrey, England and can be reached at
http://www.gillianlamb.co.uk
e-mail: gillian@gillianlamb.co.uk

Feedback and comments on this book are welcome.

Acknowledgements

I would like to thank Margaret Haigh and Mavis Woodard for supplying the beaded bracelets on page 11.

Introduction

Welcome to my first book, which I have written so that I could share the classes and workshops that I teach with everyone. This book includes my notes and diagrams that I use in these lessons together with clear pictures. There are several different main projects, as well as various "warm up" exercises and additional ideas on how to use the techniques covered in each section. When I teach I like to present to my class the "project" and then encourage everyone to make their own choices on development. It is so rewarding for me to watch each persons' interpretation and see their ideas and use of colour. So here are some of these workshops in a book for you all to enjoy. I am sure that they will give you many fun projects to work on and to experiment with.

These projects are suitable for all levels of bead enthusiast - from those who have little experience through to the experienced beader who is looking for a bit more of a challenge and a little push to try out something else.

Beginners could start with the Ogalala Lace Bracelet (p. 8) followed by the Flowers on the Net necklace (p. 16) and add some Flowers (p. 22). Afterwards why not try out rounds 1 and 5 of the Treasure Trove Necklace (p. 56, 61), before moving on to the next level?

Intermediate beaders should also start with the Ogalala Lace Bracelet (p. 8), experimenting with Flowers (p. 22)and the Flower Bracelet (p. 27). Move on to play with the Right Angle Weave Daisy Chain (p. 34) and the Rosettes (p. 50), ready to make the Marhaba necklace (p. 44) or bracelet (p. 40). Subsequently go on to to play with the techniques in the Treasure Trove Necklace (p. 52).

Those who have experience will once again enjoy the Ogalala Lace bracelet (p. 8). It is simple but very effective and has areas that can be developed to personalise it. Then, depending on your preferences, you may like to tackle the Marhaba necklace (p. 44) or bracelet (p. 40) and mix and match rounds of the Treasure Trove Necklace (p. 52) to make a very unique piece.

These are just a few suggestions, everyone has their own individual needs and inclinations. If the project is a necklace, but you never wear them, think 'How can I make this into a bracelet or can I use this for something else?' The netted necklace is a basic beading piece, but how about using different types and numbers of beads at every step – what would happen? I am trying to encourage you all to take these patterns and designs further and stretch your beading capabilities by using your own originality, and most of all to enjoy your beading creatively.

love Gillian x

Gillian

How to get the best results from this book

Materials

Beads

A variety of beads are used of different shapes and sizes in each project. They are listed at the beginning of each one. I have not given exact amounts of beads for every project – only for the Marhaba Classic Necklace. Many of these projects will actually benefit from using up small amounts of your left over beads. Blend them in with a main colour to give a continuous look. Experiment using some spare beads to test out each exercise or part of the project. You will be surprised at what can happen.

Needles

Generally, use a size 10 beading needle, but you will need to keep to hand a size 12 or 13 just in case your bead hole gets filled with thread.

Thread

I use C-Lon, Nymo, Silamide or Fireline threads, whichever I consider the best for the project I am beading. Thicknesses range from O (very fine) to AA to B to D (thicker) dependent on the type of thread used. See Notes on good beading practice below.

Conditioner

This is optional. See Notes on good beading practice below.

Good beading practice

1. Thread. Consider your thread for each project. There are many to choose from, think what the final effect is that you want to achieve. Questions to ask yourself: Do I need a thick or thin thread? Am I going through the beads just once or several times? If several times you may need to have a finer thread (and needle). Do I need to have a stiff, tightly tensioned piece (use a thicker thread) or a silky pliable effect (use a finer thread)? Do I have beads with large or small holes? If they are larger holes you may need a thicker thread.

2. Colour. Either match or choose a colour of thread to enhance your work. The colour of your thread can be seen through transparent beads and as it twists and turns in your work, so you could choose to add interest here too.

3. Conditioner. To condition or not is always a very difficult question. Everyone has their own theory. I would like to advocate 'intelligent' conditioning. Sometimes it is necessary, sometimes not. A silicon based conditioner will help to keep your thread free from tangles and give you a slinky beading effect. Wax conditioners will add a slight layer to your thread and help it grip. Both, I would suggest, should be used with care and discretion.

4. Tensioning or stopper bead. These are used to either prevent beads falling off at the start of your work or you can slide the bead up to keep the first beads tight or tensioned. It is usually a different bead from those you are using and is removed once your beads and/or the tension is secure. Go through it several times with your needle and thread, making sure that you do not split the thread as it will be difficult to remove the bead later.

5. Always leave a 20cm (8") tail when you start. This can be used later to add a clasp or stitch in.

6. Use your favourite way to add a thread, but be mindful of where you may be placing knots, just in case you need to pass through those beads again.

7. Good tension. Always try to pull your thread the way it is going through the bead, not at right angles to it, since this can loosen work. Check yourself frequently as you work, especially if you are finding your work getting looser.

8. Finally – don't forget to take a break and stretch occasionally! Stretch your back, neck, shoulders, arms, wrists and fingers. Also your eyes! Give them a break - look out of the window at a point in the distance and if they are getting sore then it is time to go for a walk in the fresh air!

How to read the diagrams

1. The red line shows you what your next move is. It shows the direction of work, which beads to pick up and which bead(s) to go through. There are also words to help you understand each step.

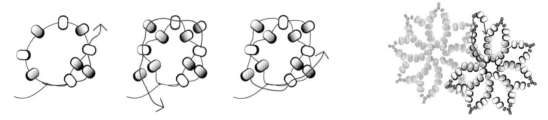

When there is a second layer of beads added to the diagram the first layer will be shown paler than it was originally drawn. This is to help with the clarity of subsequent layer(s) and to show how the layers relate to one other.

2. If you get confused as to what step you are at and what comes next, then turn the work around in your hand and match it to one of the diagrams or pictures, then try again. If you get really stuck, then do please contact me for some help.

3. Always make sure that you read all the notes – do not automatically presume that you know what is coming next!

4. Once you have followed the diagrams as set out here in the book and find that you think you could do it a different way then please do, but sometimes there is a reason why I have worked the way that I have. If you have a 'hiccup' then go back to the diagrams!

5. Do experiment with different beads, sizes and numbers. Try to stretch yourself and work out your own version of the project – I give you total permission to play!

Ogalala Lace Bracelet

This bracelet can also be made as a necklace and is an interesting and effective initial project. A very impressive result can be achieved regardless of beading experience.

You can stop after Step 6, put on a bought clasp and wear it or you can add all the interesting texture in Steps 7 and 8 and the beaded clasp to really impress you friends!

The toggle and loop are worked in peyote stitch. If you have never worked peyote stitch before I have included a short primer here for you, but do have a trial run making the loop part first with some spare beads before you work it straight onto your bracelet.

Ogalala Lace Bracelet

Materials

Size 8/0 seed beads or any bead with a large centre hole, eg double delica, for along the centre of the piece.
Size 11/0 seed beeds - colours A, B, C. Three toning colours work very well, but you could stay with all the same colour.
Pressed bead mixture of interesting shapes of small beads and perhaps some crystals to decorate with.
Thread - D thickness, providing that the hole in the centre beads is fairly large. Reduce the thickness if necessary.

Steps 1 and 2

Prepare a comfortable length of thread, as long as you can handle. Thread needle. Attach a stopper/tensioning bead.

Pick up an even number of your size 8/0 beads. Make this long enough to go around your wrist.

In this project it is better to have this length too short than too long. Turn and pick up 3 colour A size 11/0 seed beads (diag. 1).

Diag. 1

Step 3

Pick up 3A beads, miss a bead and pass through a bead.

Repeat from* to * to the end of the row.

Turn and flip your work over. Pull up the stopper bead to keep the first row tight (diag. 2).

Diag. 2

Step 4

As you bead this row your work will start to twist (diag. 3). At the turn, pick up 4A beads and pass through the central bead of the 3-bead group on the previous row.

Pick up 5B beads and pass through the central bead of the 3-bead group on the previous row.
Repeat from ** to ** to the end of the row (diag. 3).

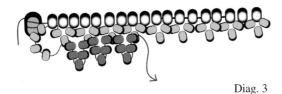

Diag. 3

Step 5

At the turn pick up 4 beads and pass through the central bead of the 5-bead group on the previous row.

Pick up 7C beads and pass through the central bead of the next 5-bead group on the previous row. Repeat from *** to *** to the end of the row (diags 4 and 5).

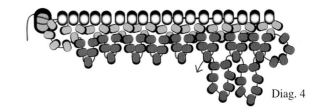

Diag. 4

Step 6

When the third netted row is completed, needle back down to your first row of large beads and repeat steps 3, 4 and 5 for a second time. You will now have two rows of twisty netting along a central bead.

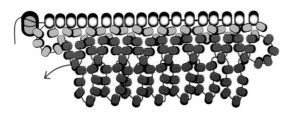

Diag. 5

Experiment!

What about adding another (4th row) to the netting, or adding some interesting beads to the last row of netting?

Tip: Try to colour blend your beads gradually from the centre to the edge.

Step 7

Once you have worked two rows of netting, return to the centre bead and pull the two layers gently apart as you work the next phase of this bracelet. The piece will be very twisty and wiggly, so go slowly and gently.

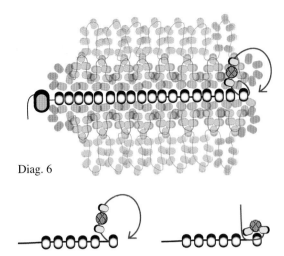

Diag. 6

Needle around until you have the thread coming out of the end bead towards the inside of the work.

Pick up several beads go around and pass back through this bead (diags 6 and 6a).

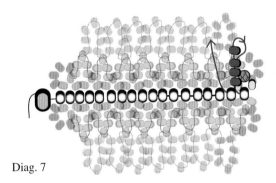

Diag. 6a

Step 8

Now work a spike.

Pick up some beads, form the spike. Then pass *forward* through the next bead (diags 7 and 7a).

Diag. 7

Repeat Steps 7 and 8 all the way along.

Sometimes you may like to work two or more spikes in the same spot. Also you may like to grade the size of your centre bead in Step 7 and spikes - making them larger towards the centre of the bracelet.

Diag. 7a

Decoration

The order of working the decoration is as follows:-

1. Make a loop around the core bead.
2. Make a spike.
3. Pass forward through the next core bead.
Repeat 1 to 3 along the centre core beads (diag. 8).

Diag. 8

Bracelet by Margaret Haigh

Finish with your thread exiting an 8/0 bead at one end, ready to add your clasp. Either add your own bought or made clasp or work the loop and toggle which follows.

Bracelet by Mavis Woodard

Peyote Toggle

Materials

Size 11/0 beads to match your work
A few size 8/0 beads
Thread and needle

Loop

Step 1

Either try this out without attaching it directly to your work or come out of one end of the central large bead column and pick up 34 beads. This number can be varied to make a smaller or larger toggle (diag. 1)

If your bracelet is a little long only pick up say 30 beads here, go around and through the first bead without leaving any beads for a stalk.

Diag. 1

Step 2

Leaving the first 4 beads (once again this number can be varied, depending on the length required) picked up out of the circle - come around and pass through the first bead again to form a circle, (bringing all the beads together, the diagram leaves gaps so that you can see the path of the thread) Don't forget to leave a reasonable length at the end to weave in if working this on its own, or bring this up close to the work if adding onto the piece (diag. 2).

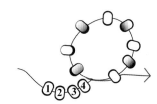

Diag. 2

Step 3

Pick up a bead, miss a bead and go through a bead.

Repeat all the way round. Keep the beads flat and fairly tight! When you pick up the last bead "step up" - that is go through the last bead of the first round and the first bead of this round! (diags 3, 4 and 5).

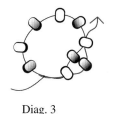

Diag. 3

Diag. 4

Diag. 5

Step 4

On this round we will go around with a size 8/0 bead to fill in each gap (diag. 6).

If you have left spare beads at the start for the stalk you will now square stitch beads to them. (See diags 7, 8 and 9.)

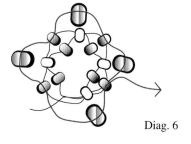

Diag. 6

Square stitch beads for the stalk together like this: once you have placed the last size 8/0 bead, needle around until the thread is coming out of a bead in a direction ready to work down the spare beads for a stalk. Your work may not look exactly as shown. Find your own path, but do not leave any thread showing (diag. 7).

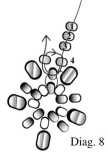

Diag. 7

Pick up one 11/0 bead. Attach to the fourth bead picked up at step 1. Come back through a bead in the loop if there is space (diag. 8).

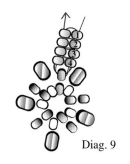

Diag. 8

Repeat for all 4 beads. Take thread back into centre row of bracelet and secure neatly (diag. 9).

Diag. 9

12

Peyote Toggle

Materials

Size 11/0 beads to match your work
A few size 8/0 beads
Thread and needle

Toggle
Step 1

Make a small peyote tube for the toggle to go through the loop. Pick up 13 beads. Do not pick up another bead! Miss two beads and go through the next bead. Pick up a bead, miss a bead, go through a bead all the way to the end (diags 1 and 2).

Diag. 1   Diag. 2

Step 2

Pull both threads tightly to arrange the beads as seen in diag. 3. Turn your work. Now look for all the high beads These are the beads to go through on the next row.

Diag. 3

Peyote back and forth for a total of 12 rows. Remember to count the rows diagonally. See diagrams below.

These diagrams show two different ways of counting your peyote rows.
The number of rows shown in each diagram is 6.

Step 3

Pick up a bead, pass through a bead all the way to the end (diag. 4).

Diag. 4

Pick up 17 beads to start

Pick up 13 beads to start

A longer toggle bar can be made by using more beads in the first pick up.

Zip up

Bring the first row around and join it to the last row. The beads will fit into one another like a zip. Needle through from one side to the other until all are joined. Remember to go and join the last bead you exit too.

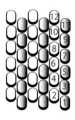

Now cover the thread on the end by picking up a bead and passing under the loop all the way around. If you wish, put a size 8/0 bead into the middle, then needle around all the edge beads again, pulling them in together.

Finally, needle down to the other end and repeat. Once this is done, needle your thread to the middle of the toggle ready to attach it to your work. To neaten the starting thread, needle up from the other end into the centre. These two threads will be used to attach the toggle to the bracelet.

End on view of tube

Flowers on the Net

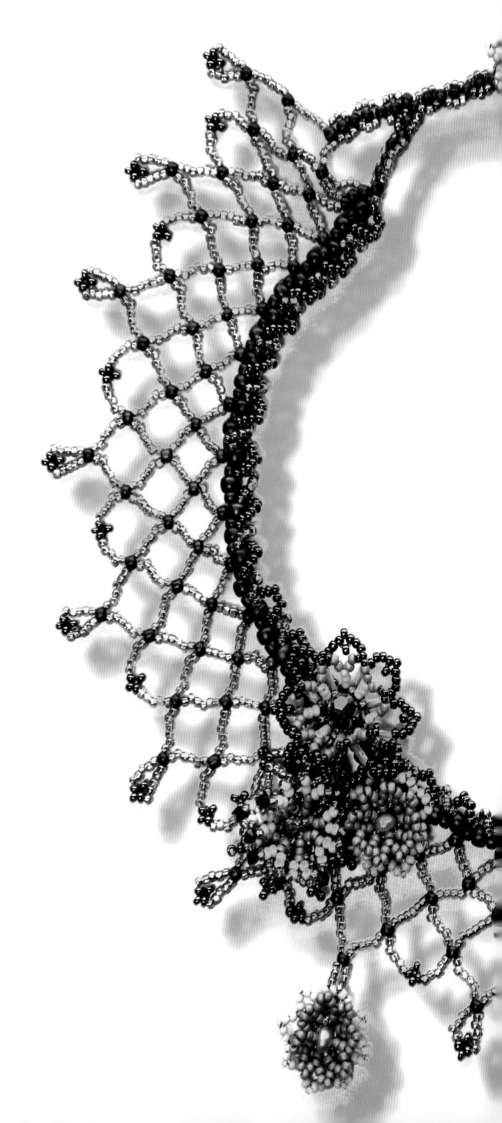

I put this design together to make a special netted necklace because I could not find one in a book at that time. Try out different types (and numbers) of beads at all stages to come up with something very different. Then add some flowers from the next chapter to personalise it.

This necklace is made up of a decorated core of beads from which a lattice or netted skirt is worked. Flowers are added to decorate as required.

The order of working is as follows:

1.   Core
2.   Lattice skirt
3.   Decorate the core
4.   Adjust the length and add a clasp. Try using Right Angle Weave Daisy Chain (see page 34).
5.   Make and add flowers as desired from the Flowers section (page 22).

I have also included another way of making a netted necklace. It is quite fun to try it out and also for practising manoeuvring your needle around the top edge before adding more beads. Do try out a small piece even if you don't want to make a whole necklace from this technique.

Flowers on the Net Necklace

Introduction

This necklace is made up of a decorated core of beads from which a lattice skirt is worked. Flowers are added to decorate as required.

The order of working is as follows:
1. The core
2. Lattice skirt
3. Decorate the core
4. Adjust the length and add a clasp
5. Make and add the flowers.

Materials

Seed beads
Size 11/0 - 2 colours, A & C
Size 8/0 – colour B
Size 6/0 – colour D
Thread "D" thickness
Needle, size 10

Step 1 - The core

Prepare a comfortable length of thread, two stretched arms widths if you can manage the length, *plus* extra thread to leave at the beginning. This will be used later to finish, add length or add a clasp.

Thread the needle. Do not knot.

Step 2

Leave a good length of thread, then carefully add a stopper or tensioning bead (see introductory notes.)

Now pick up 1B and 1D bead alternately for the length you require. You don't have to be exact since the length may be adjusted from the other end later if necessary.

Finish the pick up with 5B beads (diag. 1).

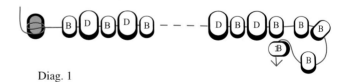

Diag. 1

The Lattice Skirt

Steps 3 to 9 show the making of the lattice part of the necklace. You may want this only on the front of your necklace - or maybe a little further around your neck, draping over your shoulders.

Step 3

First pick up for the lattice skirt

4A, 1B, 4A, 1B, 6A, 1B, 6A, 1B, 5A and 4C

This is very long - it sets the depth of the skirt (diag. 2).

Step 4

Next make a berry. Take the needle through beads 1, 2 and 3 of the colour C beads. Pull carefully into shape (diags 3 and 3a).

Step 5

It may be more comfortable to turn your work now. Work up the other side of step 3.
Pick up 5A, pass through 1B.
Pick up 6A, 1B, 6A. Pass through 1B.
Pick up 4A, 1B, 4A Pass through beads marked W, X, Y and Z (diag. 4).

Step 6

Pick up 1B, 4A, pass through 1B.
Pick up 4A, 1B, 6A. Pass through 1B.
Pick up 5A, 4C. Make a berry as in Step 4 (diag. 5).

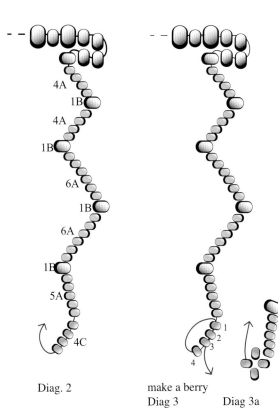

Diag. 2

make a berry
Diag 3   Diag 3a

Diag. 4

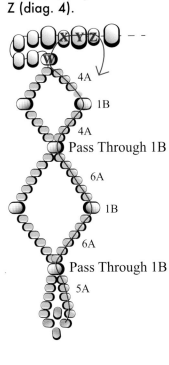

Diag. 5

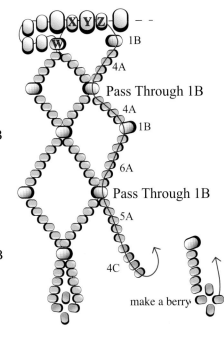

Diag. 6

Step 7

Pick up 5A, 1B, 6A pass through 1B.
Pick up 4A, 1B, 4A, pass through beads marked W, X, Y and Z in diag. 6.

Step 8

Pick up 1B, 4A, pass through 1B.
Pick up 4A, 1B, 6A, pass through 1B.
Pick up 6A, 1B, 5A, 4C Make a berry (diag. 7).

Diag. 7

make a berry (see Diag. 3 and 3a)

Step 9

Work along the large core beads repeating steps 4, 5, 6, 7 and 8 for the length required.

NB Don't forget to pick up 1B bead at the start of steps 6 and 8!

Adjust the length as necessary.

Make sure you work the end to match the start.

Then when happy start the embellishment of the core beads.

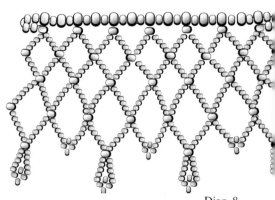

Diag. 8

Decorate the core beads

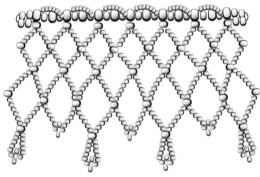

Diag. 9

Step 10

Come out through the front of a D bead. Pick up 7A beads. Miss a D bead. Go through the back of the next D bead. Repeat this from * to * to the end (diag. 9).

Step 11

Work back along the row this way

**Come out of the back of a D bead. Pick up 8C beads.

Go through the front of the next D bead.** Repeat from ** to ** to the end (diag. 10).

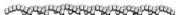

The loops intertwine across the top. Bead numbers in each loop may need to be adjusted for best effect.

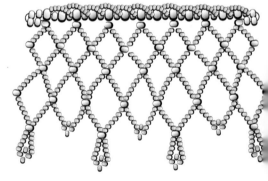

Diag 10

Nearly there! Adjust the length...

To make your necklace the correct length, work a section of Right Angle Weave Chain (see page 34) on each side of the netting (picture below).

If you prefer you could simply thread on more core beads before adding a clasp, but don't forget to reinforce the beads just added should you choose this option.

and ... add a clasp

When you make the flowers stitch one over the clasp. But do make sure that you can still open and close the clasp!

Finally!

Decorate the necklace with flowers if desired.

Make a selection of these from the Flowers section in this book (p. 22).

When making flowers to decorate your necklace here are a few things to remember:

1. For best effect make sure that the colour you choose for the petals of your flowers stands out from that used in the netted necklace. If you used a shiny bead for the netting, choose an opaque one for the flower and/or outline your petals with another colour.
2. Make a variety of flowers in different sizes, colours and layers.
3. Make a few flowers exactly the same to give continuity.

Temporarily tack your flowers onto your necklace. Put it around your neck and check their placement in the mirror.

Once you are happy with the result sew them on permanently, neaten all ends and your necklace is finished!

Lattice Necklace

An alternative way of making this project is to make the core and the skirt together. With this method you will have more control over the length of the necklace.

Use a variety of colours, sizes and shapes of beads. Those used in these diagrams are for clarity.

Step 1

Follow diagrams 1 to 6. This makes 4 circles of beads.

Diag. 1

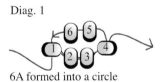

6A formed into a circle

Diag. 2

5A

Diag. 3

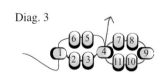

Diag. 4

5B

Diag. 5

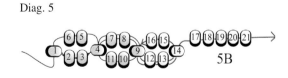

5B

Diag. 6

Diag. 7

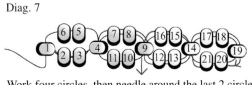

Work four circles, then needle around the last 2 circles and bring thread back down out of the bead.

Step 2

Make the drop for the skirt by picking up the beads shown in diag. 8.

First Drop Segment
Pick up 1B, 5A, 1B, 5A, 1B, 6A, 1B, 5A, 4C.
Make a berry (see p. 17). Then pick up 5A, pass through 1B.
Pick up 6A, 1B, 5A, pass through 1B.
Pick up 5A, 1B. Pass through the end bead of the last circle (diag. 8).

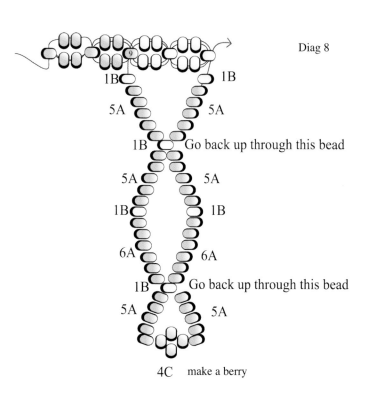

Diag 8

1B   1B

5A   5A

1B   Go back up through this bead

5A   5A

1B   1B

6A   6A

1B   Go back up through this bead

5A   5A

4C   make a berry

Add two more circles to the top row (diags 3–6).

Needle through beads X, Y and Z ready to start the next drop (diag. 9).

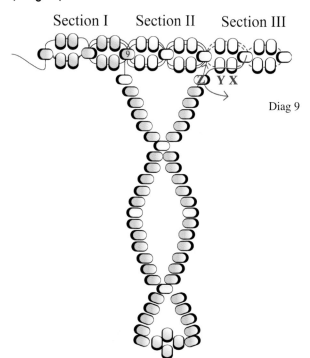

Section I   Section II   Section III

Z Y X

Diag 9

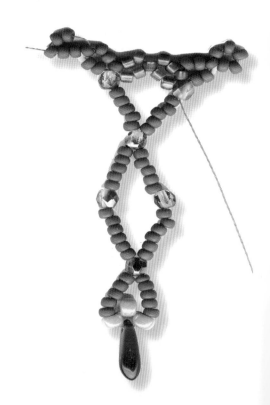

Step 3

Second Drop Segment
Pick up 5A, 1B, 5A, pass through 1B.
Pick up 5A, 4C, make a berry.
Pick up 5A, 1B, 5A, pass through 1B.
Pick up 5A, 1B, pass through the end bead of the
last circle (diag. 10).

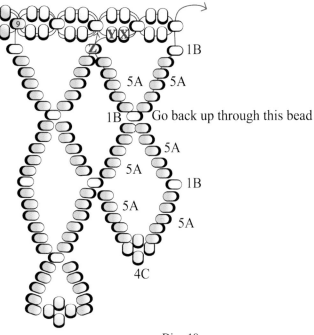

1B

5A 5A

1B Go back up through this bead

5A

5A

1B

5A

5A

4C

Diag 10

Step 4

**Add two more circles to the top row (diag. 9).
First Drop Segment
Pick up 5A, 1B, 5A, pass through 1B
Pick up 6A, 1B, 5A, 4C. Make a berry. Then pick up 5A, pass
through 1B.
Pick up 6A, 1B, 5A, pass through 1B.
Pick up 5A, 1B pass through the end bead of the last circle.
Second Drop Segment
Work as in diag 10**

Repeat from ** to ** for length required.

Step 5

When long enough add a further two circles at the top to
match the start and then decorate the circles with loops of
beads.

Add a clasp and neaten all ends.

Add flowers if desired.

Experiment!

Experiment with different types and
sizes of beads to make a really
interesting necklace. How can you
vary the top circles and decoration?

Flowers

Flowers

These are the flowers that I first used on the netted necklace. They are fun and can be used on their own to make many things. Master each type and make earrings or decorations for bags and clothes.

Make one type and repeatedly join them together to make a bracelet or necklace. Or layer several types together as in the Glitzy Ring, which also uses the Right Angle Weave Daisy Chain for the ring band.

Right Angle Weave Flower

Flowers and circular motifs

By using a combination of beads for each side you can obtain a circular motif.

The bottom (b) = one seed bead ⬤
The top (t) = 5 seed beads ⬤⬤⬤⬤⬤
The sides(s) = 4 seed beads ⬤⬤⬤⬤   or you could use a 3mm or 6mm bugle bead
Try out other combinations using bugle beads, seeds size 8/0 and size 15/0, for example.

Materials

Size 11/0, 8/0 or 15/0 seed beads
3mm or 6mm bugle beads

Step 1

Start by picking
up b, s, t, s and go
through the b and
s to form a circle
(diag. 1).

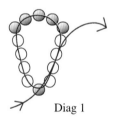

Diag 1

Step 2

Now pick up t, s and b and go up
through the previous side. Go on through
the t beads you just picked up, then back
down through the s beads you picked up
last (diag. 2).

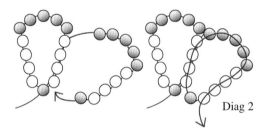

Diag 2

Step 3

Pick up b, s and t, and go down
through the previous side. Go on
through the b bead picked up last and
back up through the s beads you just
picked up (diag. 3).

Diag 3

Repeat Steps 2 and 3 until you have only one top segment to make. Depending on the number of segments - you can have an odd or even number of segments. Whatever you want the circle to look like!

When you are ready to close your flower, check which bead your thread is coming out of and then proceed to Step 4.

Step 4

If you are at the bottom of a petal, pick up a base bead and go up the side beads. Finally pick up the petal's top edge beads and go down the side bead. If you are at the top of the petal you are coming up a set of s beads. Pick up your t beads and pass back down the very first set of s beads to join the circle up. Then pick up your centre bead to complete the flower (diag. 4).

 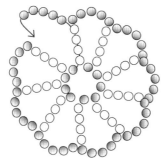

Diag. 4

Step 5

Sew a crystal or other feature bead into the centre of you flower - or add another layer. To make this easier use a bead with a larger hole for the base bead. Finish off all ends and then why not experiment?

Experiment!

Experiment with types, colours and numbers of beads.

Flower 2

This is a very useful flower. It is made using a needle at each end of your thread. Petals are made alternately with each needle. Add an extra layer and if you vary the number and type of beads used in each petal you can get some very individual looking flowers.

Materials

Seed beads
Size 11/0 - 2 colours A and B
Size 15/0 - colour C
(or you could use another size 11/0)
Needle and thread to match.

Step 1

Pick up 1A, 1B and repeat until you have 10 beads on your thread.

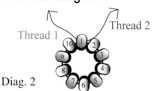
Diag. 1

Step 2

Make a circle and go through bead 1 again. Push beads into the centre of your thread. Put a needle on the other end. Work should look like diag. 2.

Diag. 2

Petal 1
Step 3

Using thread 1, pick up 6A, 3B, 3C beads.

Step 4

Go back through the second C bead picked up (diag. 3).

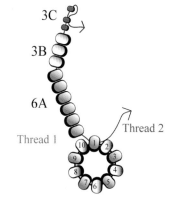
Diag. 3

Step 5

Pick up 1C, 3B, 6A beads.

Go through the next bead in the base circle. (The first time it is bead 2). From left to right (diag. 4).

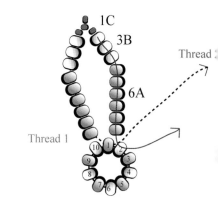
Diag. 4

Petal 2 and next 7 petals
Step 6

Using thread 2 (or change threads).

Go up through the last 6A of the previous petal. Pick up 3B and 3C beads (diag. 5).

Repeat steps 4 and 5.

Pick up thread 1. Repeat step 6 alternating between threads all the way around your base circle until 9 petals have been worked.

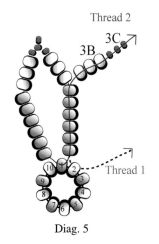
Diag. 5

Making the last petal
Step 7

Change threads. Go up through the last 6A of the previous petal.

Pick up 3B, 3C beads. Go back through the second C bead picked up. Pick up 1C, 3B.

Go back down the 6A beads of the first petal made (diag. 6).

Finish off the ends of thread or go around again and make another layer, only this time use fewer beads in each section of each petal.

Diag. 6

The two pictures on the left show the back and front of a multiple layered flower.

Below is a pointsettia made by using different numbers and beads as you work each petal.

Flower Bracelet

There is another way to work Flower 2 with only one needle. It is simple and quick and similar to the way that Flower 1 is worked. By using this method and changing the numbers of beads picked up you can make a very pretty bracelet.

Materials

Seed beads
Size 11/0 - 2 colours A and B
Size 15/0 C (or you could use another size 11/0)
Needle and thread to match. Fine thread is good since we are using size 15/0 beads for the picots

Step 1

Use as much thread as you can comfortably manage.

Pick up 1A, 1B and repeat until you have 8 beads on your thread.

Step 2

Make a circle and go through bead 1 again. Leave a good length tail to weave in later - or add a catch (diag. 1).

Diag. 1

Step 3 Petal

Pick up 3A, 2B and 3C beads.

Step 4

Go back through the second C bead picked up (diag. 2).

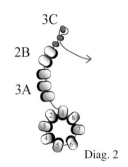

Diag. 2

Step 5

Pick up 1C, 2B and 3A beads. Come around and back through bead 1, then pass through bead 2 in the base circle (diag. 3).

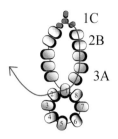

Diag. 3

Step 6

(Repeat all of this until the last petal.)

Petal 2 and next 6 petals

Repeat steps 3 and 4 (diag. 4).

Pick up 1C and 2B. Pass down through the nearest 3A beads of the last petal worked (diag. 5)

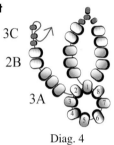

Diag. 4

Diag. 5

Step 7 Making the last petal

When you have 7 points, pass up through the next set of 3A beads.

Pick up 2B and 3A. Make the picot, pick up 1C and 2B. Pass down through 3A beads to complete the flower (diag. 6).

Diag. 6

Step 8

Now needle through beads to the point of a picot, then pick up 8 beads as in Step 1.

Step 9

Work 6 petals as before – ignore the small picot bead.

Step 11

Work a final petal, laying it on top of the previous flower. Pass needle through beads around to the opposite side and make another flower. Keep repeating this until it is long enough to go around the wrist. You could make a necklace too.

Step 10

On the next petal pick up 3A, 2B and 2C. Pass through nearest picot bead of previous flower. Pick up 1C and 2B and finish the petal (diag. 7).

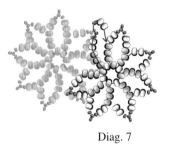

Diag. 7

NB you could also place a small bead in the centre of each flower as you work. Finish off the ends of the thread. Add a clasp or use an unfinished flower and loop as a closure.

Flower 3

An interesting flower which can be played with and all sorts of variations made. Once again don't forget to add an extra layer or vary the number and type of beads used.

Materials

Seed beads
2 colours A and B (try using a size 8/0 for A and a size 11/0 for B)
Needle and thread to match.

Step 1

Make a circle of 9A beads. Tie a knot and bring needle through bead 1 (diag. 1).

Diag. 1

Step 2

Pick up 1B, 6A, 3B.

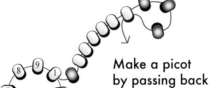

Make a picot by passing back down through first A bead from needle (diag. 2).

Diag. 2

Step 3

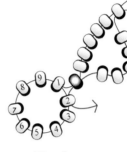

Pick up 5A. Pass down through B bead nearest the centre circle and then through bead 2 (diag. 3).

Diag. 3

Step 4

Pick up 1B, 2A. Pass up through centre A bead of group picked up in Step 3, marked X in diag. 4.

Diag. 4

Step 5

Pick up 3A, 3B (diag. 5).

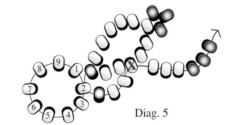

Diag. 5

Step 6 onwards

Repeat Steps 2 to 5 moving around the centre circle beads until you come out of the last bead in the circle.

Complete the flower. Come out of the last bead in the circle. Work Step 4 (diag. 6).

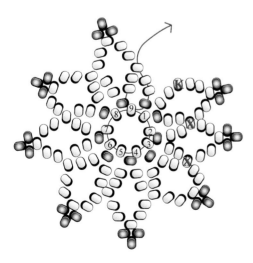

Diag. 6

Diag. 7

Make a picot as in Step 2. Pick up 2A. Pass back through bead K to complete the flower. Work thread back into the centre. Finish off all ends (diag. 7).

Glitzy Ring
First layer

This fun ring is made in three layers.

Materials

The first layer combination is as follows:

The centre (C) = one size 11/0 seed bead

The side (S) = is a combination of 2 x 6mm bugle beads square stitched together. This is explained below but the finished side looks like this

The edge (E) is a combination of 11/0 and 15/0 seed beads, explained below, but the finished top looks like this

Try out other combinations for the sides and top such as 3mm bugle beads, size 8/0s and so on.

Step 1

We start by making the side combination.

Pick up 2 bugles and square stitch them together. Now turn this around to resemble diag. 1.

Diag. 1

Step 2

Pick up the C bead, 1 bugle (S) and now we will make the edge section. Pick up 2 size 11/0 and 4 size 15/0s. Go back through the first size 15/0 bead picked up. Pick up 2 size 11/0 beads (diag. 2).

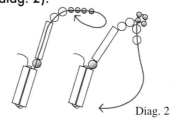

Diag. 2

Step 3

Pass up through the first side bugle, the C bead and the second side bugle.

Arrange to look like diag. 3.

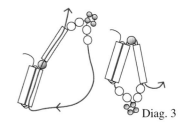

Diag. 3

Step 4

Pull everything together tightly and arrange neatly as in the diagram.

Pick up 1 S bugle and square stitch to the other S bugle (diag. 4).

Diag. 4

Experiment!

Experiment with types, colours and numbers of beads.

Step 5

Repeat Steps 2, 3 and 4 until you have only one edge segment to make (diag. 5).

You can have an odd or even number of segments – whatever you want the circle to look like!

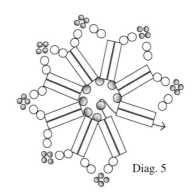

Diag. 5

Pick up 1C bead. Pass up through the S bugle.

Pick up 2E 11/0s and 4E 15/0s. Make the edge picots as before. Pick up 2 E11/0s.

Complete the circle by going down the next S bugle and you've finished this round (diags 5 and 6).

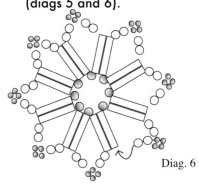

Diag. 6

Second layer -

Materials

The second layer combination is as follows:
The centre (C) = one size 11/0 seed bead
The side (S) = is a 6mm bugle
The edge (E) = is made of five 11/0 seed beads

Step 6

Now we put one seed bead in between each C bead of the first layer. Pull them in tightly (diag. 7).

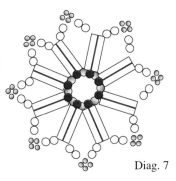

Diag. 7

The second layer starts with this ring of seed beads. Exit from one of these beads (diag. 8).

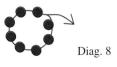

Diag. 8

These seed beads will be used as the C or centre bead for the next layer. For clarity I will show only the second layer in the next set of diagrams.

Step 7

Pick up beads for S, E and S. Go around and back through the C bead you first came out of and the first S bead just picked up (diag. 9).

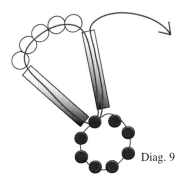

Diag. 9

Step 8

Pick up beads for E and S. Go around and back through the next C bead in the ring, the S bead (that was already there) and the E and S beads just picked up.

Go around again through the C, S, E and S beads and then pass through the next C in the ring (diag. 10).

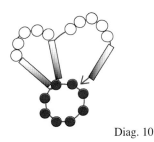

Diag. 10

Step 9

Pick up beads for S and E. Go around and back down through the previous S bead in the ring, the C bead and the S bead just picked up (diag. 11).

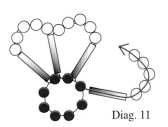

Diag. 11

Repeat Steps 8 and 9 all the way around your C beads.

Don't forget that for your last petal you will only have to pick up the edge beads and join them in.

Remember to go through your last centre bead. Pull everything fairly tight! Tie a knot if it helps.

Step 10

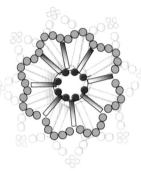

Diag. 12

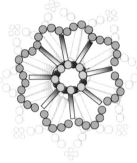

Diag. 13

Diag. 13a

The second layer is now complete and will look like the picture above.

In diagram 12 it is shown on top of the first layer.

Now place one seed bead in between each C bead of the second layer. Pull them in tightly (diag. 13).

These are the beads to use for the centre of the third and final layer (diag. 13a).

Third Layer

The third layer starts with this ring of seed beads shown in diag. 13a.

Exit from one of these beads as before, but *be careful*. The petals in the third round are worked differently from those in rounds 1 and 2!

Materials

Start here - Step 11

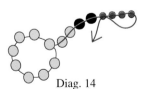

Diag. 14

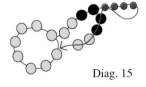

Diag. 15

The second layer combination is as follows:
Size 11/0 seed beads A
Size 11/0 seed beads B
Size 15/0 seed beads C

Pick up 2A, 2B and 4C.
Pass back through the fourth C bead (diag. 14).

Pick up 2B and 2A.
Pass back through the next A bead in the centre ring (diag. 15).

Step 12

Work steps A, B and C around your centre beads (diags 16a, b and c).

Come out of the centre bead. Pass back through the last 2A beads picked up (diag. 16a).

Pick up 2B and 4C. Make a picot as in Step 11 (diag. 16b).

Pick up 2B and 2A. Pass back through the next A bead in the centre ring (diag. 16c)

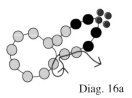

Diag. 16a

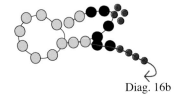

Diag. 16b

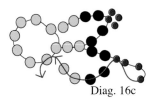

Diag. 16c

You will end up with a layer a bit like this... yours too may look irregular!

To finish the flower, stitch a crystal across the middle.

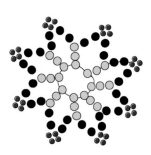

To turn this into a ring - add a band. Use the Right Angle Weave Daisy Chain (page 34).

Make a sufficient length to go around your finger, include the width of your flower.

Attach to each side of your flower. It is probably better to have your ring slightly too tight than too loose.

On completion you can if you choose go back and add some bugle beads or daggers pointing outwards, in between layers 2 and 3.

Why not play with the pattern for the band and make a bracelet or necklace to match...?

...or make a ring out of the band.

Try adding some drop beads as you work. What happens?

Right Angle Weave
Daisy Chain

This is such a fun and versatile thing to make. I have used 'Pick up One' to add a small strap addition to the Flowers on the Net Necklace and to add a band to the Glitzy Ring.

Try out 'Pick up Two'. Play with this by using different beads and you will be surprised at the different effects that you can achieve.

In mastering this pick-up you will learn the basis of the Marhaba necklace and bracelet.

Make these little bracelets and matching necklaces from the Right Angle Weave Daisy Chain. Use 'Pick up Two' and substitute Magatama beads or drop beads, which have their holes offset to one side for the Squares.

Be ready to experiment with other combinations!

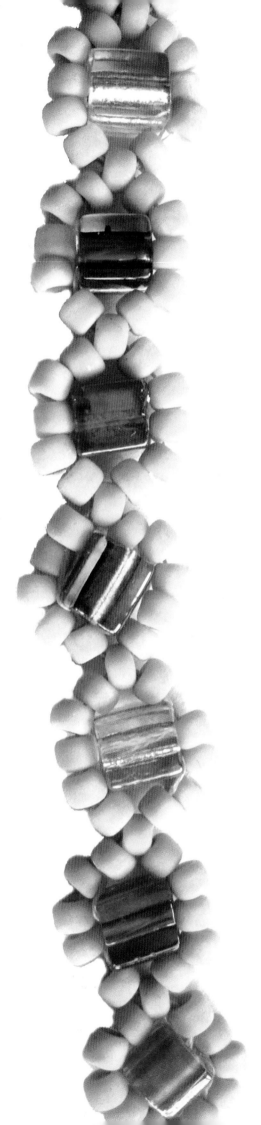

Daisy Chain

You can start this by using seed beads of two sizes and then go on to play with different combinations of beads.

Materials

Seed Beads :- Sizes 11/0 (A)
8/0 (B)
Squares
Hexs size 8/0
Pressed beads sizes 4mm; 6mm

Pick up one

Using just the A (A) and B (B) beads

Pick up alternate A and B beads. Go back through them all (diag. 1).	Pick up 1A, 1B and 1A. Go around and up your last B bead (diag. 2).	Pass back through the first A and B beads just picked up (diag. 3).	Pull beads together so that they look like those in diag. 4.	Pick up 1A, 1B and 1A. Go around and down your last B bead. Pass back through the first 2 beads just picked up (diag. 5).

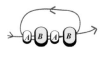

Diag. 1

Diag. 2

Diag. 3

Diag. 4

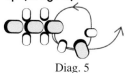

Diag. 5

Variation A - one bead in-fill

Start by exiting a B bead.

Go through the next A bead. Pick up 1A bead.

Go through the next A bead and down through the next B bead, then A bead.

Pick up 1A bead.

Go through the next A bead and up through the next B bead, then A bead (diag. 6).

Once this embellishment is completed repeat back again.

You will find that you fill in the gap on each side of the band with more A beads forming a flower look (diag. 7).

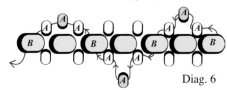

Diag. 6

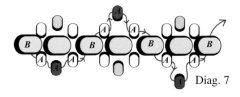

Diag. 7

Variation B - two bead in-fill

Start by exiting a B bead.

Go through the next A bead.

Pick up 2A beads.

Go through the next A bead and down through the next B bead, then the next A bead.

Pick up 2A beads.

Go through the next A bead and up through the next B bead, then the next A bead (diag. 8).

Once this embellishment is completed repeat back again.

You will find that you fill in the gap on each side of the band with more A beads forming a "flower" look (diag. 9).

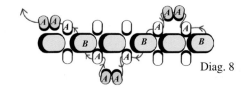

Diag. 8

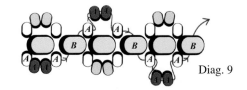

Diag. 9

Now try out other combinations of beads

Materials

Squares ⬜

Hexs size 8/0 ⬡

Pressed Beads sizes 4mm ⬤

6mm ⬤

Using the ⬜ and ⬡ work through Variation B on page 36 again.

Pick up two

First try this using just the Ⓐ and ⬜ beads

Pick up the beads shown below and go back through them all (diag. 1).	Turn your work on its side to look like diag. 2.	Make sure you are coming out of a ⬜ bead (diag. 3).	Pick up 3A beads. Go around and up your last ⬜ bead (diag. 4).	Pass back through the first 2A beads just picked up (diag. 5).

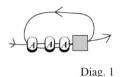

Diag. 1

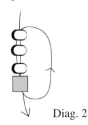

Diag. 2

Diag. 3

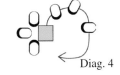

Diag. 4

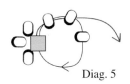

Diag. 5

Pull beads together so that they look like those in diag. 6.

Pick up 1A, 1 square bead and 1A. Go around and down the centre A bead you came out of (diag. 7).

Repeat from Diags 4 to 7 for the length required.

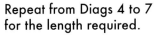

When you have the required length, go back and embellish with beads. Come through a seed bead on the end, then another seed. Pick up 2 seed beads, go through a seed bead, etc (see previous page). You are embellishing around the square bead.

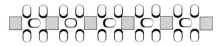

Diag. 6

Diag. 7

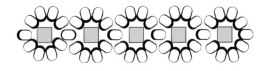

Next substitute hex beads for the size 11/0 seed beads and you get this:

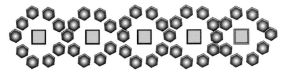

A good combination of beads to use are size 11/0 beads together with drop or Magatama beads.

Now substitute in 4mm pressed beads and size 8/0 beads alternately and you get this:

Finally using Pick up Two and Variation B, try to work out how to change colours to obtain the serpentine effect.

Marhaba

Marhaba

This beautiful and versatile necklace and bracelet was originally designed while on holiday in Tunisia, staying at the Marhaba Beach Hotel - 'Marhaba' is the Arabic word for 'Hello' or 'Welcome'.

A single strand of the bracelet will also make a very classy necklace; just try out as many combinations of beads as you can think of.

Here are a few hints and tips for choosing supplies for Marhaba

Marhaba Bracelet – Version 1

Size 11/0 seed beads – 15 to 20gms
Pressed cut glass beads 4mm – 60 approx
Size 12 needle
Nymo B
For the clasp – extra 4mm beads or matching size 8/0 beads

Marhaba Bracelet – Version 2

(Recommended for experienced beaders only.)

8gm tube of size 15/0 seed beads
Approx. 100 3mm Swarovski
Bicone crystals (mix two tones/colours if you like)
Size 12 or 13 needle
Nymo, B or finer
Amounts are approximate and depend on the length of bracelet to be made.
Take great care when making this bracelet, since the holes fill with thread and when using the glass crystals they may cut the thread. This version can be a real challenge, but worth the effort!

Necklace – Classic Marhaba

Size 11/0 seed beads – 30gms. To get the best results for this necklace use rounded Japanese size 11/0 seed beads since they sit together better.
Pressed cut glass beads 6mm – 30
Pressed cut glass beads 4mm – 60
Nymo B, colour to match 4mm beads. The thread here is very important. This technique requires the thread to pass through one bead (size 11/0) several times. Any other thread will cause problems, particularly if it is thicker.
Use a size 10 needle but have on hand a finer size 12 or 13 in case it is needed.
Colours used in the original Classic:
11/0 Miyuki – Colour 228
Pressed cut glass beads, both sizes – black.

Original and Sea Marhaba are developments of the Classic pattern. Try out different beads to get some stunning effects.

Necklace – Sea Marhaba

Size 11/0 seed Beads – 20gms
Size 8/0 seed beads – 10gms
Pressed cut glass beads 4mm – 65
Pressed glass small daggers – 35
Size 10 or 12 needle
Nymo B, colour to match 4mm beads

Necklace – Original Marhaba

Size 11/0 hexagonal beads – 20 to 30gms (I used three different colours)
Pressed cut glass beads 4mm – 70
Size 10 or 12 needle
Nymo B, colour to match 4mm beads

Amounts for all necklaces are approximate and depend on the final length.
The Rosettes and Half Rosettes make great earrings or make a large one into a brooch. See what you can come up with!

Marhaba – Classic Bracelet

Materials

Amounts depend on the length that you require, but these amounts should be sufficient

Seed beads: size 11/0 at least 10 grams or size 15/0

Approx 30 pressed beads size 4mm, or 100 crystals size 3mm

Chain – First Row

Pick up 3A and 1B bead. Go back through them all (diag. 1).

Arrange your work so that it looks like diag. 2.

Pick up 3A beads. Go around and up through the B bead (diag. 3).

Pass through 2A beads (diag. 4).

Pick up 1A, 1B and 1A bead (diag. 5).

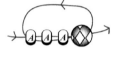

Diag. 1

Diag. 2

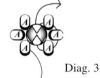

Diag. 3

Diag. 4

Diag. 5

Pass down through the A bead you were coming out of (diag. 6).

Pass through the next A and B bead (diag. 7).

Repeat from diags 3 to 7 for the length required, ending after Step 4.

When you have the required length, go back and embellish with type A beads.

Think about the type of catch you will add to this bracelet. Do not forget to leave space for a catch, it is easier to lengthen than to shorten!

Diag. 6

Diag. 7

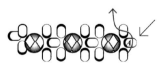

Diag. 8

Start here
Come through the centre A bead, then through the next A bead (diag. 8).

Diag.9

Pick up 5A beads (diag. 9).

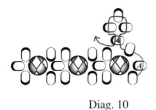 Pass down through the fourth bead from the needle end, to make a Picot (diag. 10).

Diag. 10

 Pick up 1A, pass through the next A bead.

Pass down through the central A bead of the group and the next A.

Diag. 11

Repeat from diags 9 to 11 all the way along alternate edges of your chain. When you get to the end of the first row turn and work diags 9 to 11 again in all the empty gaps as shown below in diags 12 and 13.

Turn

Bring your thread through the next 2A beads as in diag. 12.

Now work back along this side, working picots as before (diag.13).

Diag. 12

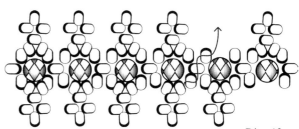

Diag.13

Put the completed first row to one side

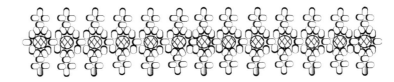

Row 2

Now make another chain of the same length as row 1, but only work diagrams 1 to 8 for the same length as for row 1 of the bracelet (diag. 14).

Bring your needle round and out of row 2 ready to decorate as before (diag. 15).

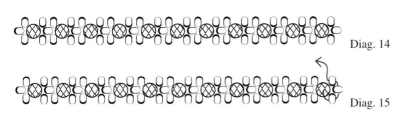

Diag. 14

Diag. 15

Now join the two pieces together!

Bringing the rows together

Bring both rows together and start to join like this:

Holding row 2 up to row 1

Step 1

Pick up 1A bead. Go through the centre bead of the peak on row 1, marked x.

Pick up 1A bead. Go down through the diagonal on row 2 as usual (diag. 4).

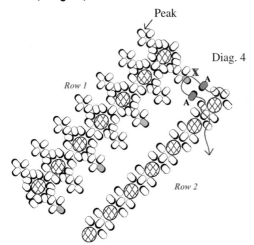

Step 2

Work a peak on the outer edge of row 2 as before. See diags 9, 10 and 11.

Pass thread up through diagonal of row 2 as usual (diag. 5).

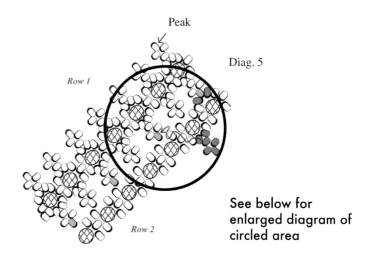

See below for enlarged diagram of circled area

Step 2 back to Step 1 – enlarged

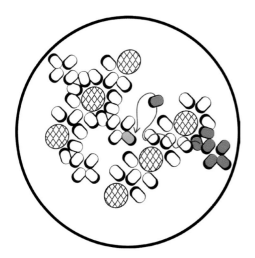

Work steps 1 and 2 all the way along, joining the two rows together. Now turn at the end, needle around and work back joining as before in Step 1 and Step 2, filling in the gaps.

The pink beads represent those added in the first pass of joining row 1 to row 2. The green beads represent those added in the second pass of joining row 1 to row 2.

Neaten all ends and add a clasp.

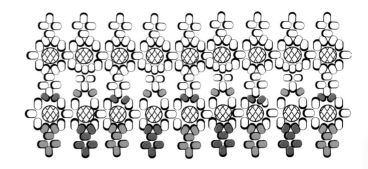

The Clasp

Bobble

You need to work the bobble first so that you can make the loop fit properly. The original for this was worked with 3mm Swarovski crystals and size 15/0 seed beads. It is a good idea to try this out with larger beads first! Try 4mm crystals and size 11/0 seeds. You need to make sure that everything is held tightly together, but not so tightly that you snap your thread. See what other combinations of beads work together.

Step 1

Make sure that your thread is coming out of an end bead, you may already have a thread in this area. Thread it up and work into position (diag. 1).

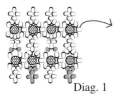

Diag. 1

Step 2

Pick up 6A (for the stalk) once. Now pick up 1B and 2A four times. This will go around to make the bobble (diag. 2).

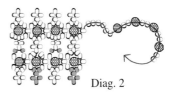

Diag. 2

Step 3

Pass needle through the first crystal picked up and continue through 2A, 1B, 2A. Pull together tightly to form a square (diags 3 and 4).

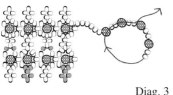

Diag. 3   Diag. 4

Step 4

Pick up 2B (diag. 5).

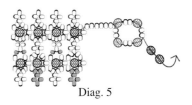

Diag. 5

Step 5

Take the needle across the circle and go down through 2A and 1B (diag. 6).

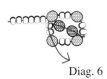

Diag. 6

Step 6

Pick up 1B. Loop the thread around thread in the centre of the 2B beads just added across the diagonal (diags 7 and 8).

Diag. 7   Diag. 8

Step 7

Pick up another B and go through the opposite B and 2A beads from left to right (diag. 9).

Diag. 9

Turn the bobble over and repeat Steps 4 to 7 on the other side. Everything will look back to front, so think carefully about where you are going!

Diag. 10

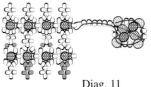

Diag. 11

Finally go around the outer edge of the bobble to reinforce. Then come back down the 6 stalk beads into the bracelet and finish off your thread (diags 10 and 11). Make another to match on row 2.

The Loop

Now you have the size of your bobbles you can make the loops.

Come out of Row 1 through the centre bead.
Pick up about 11A (size 15/0), 1B and 11A.
Go back through the bead above the central one you started from (diag. 12)
Check that this is the correct fit!

This can be tricky. Too loose and the bracelet falls off, too tight and you end up wriggling the crystals on the thread of the bobble to enable them to go through the loop.

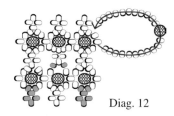

Diag. 12

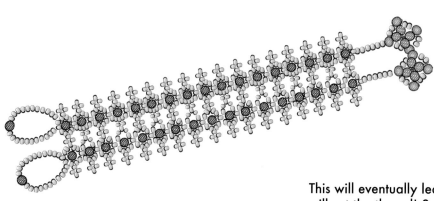

This will eventually lead to tragedy as they are very sharp and will cut the thread! So take a little time to get this right! When you are happy work the thread around the loop as many times as you can. Then take it into the bracelet and finish off as usual. Make another on Row 2.

Marhaba - Classic Necklace

Materials

Amounts depend on the length that you require, but these amounts should be sufficient

Size 11/0 seed beads Ⓐ at least 25 grams

Pressed beads sizes 4mm ⊕ 6mm ⊛ Approx 70 size 4mm and 35 size 6mm

The Chain

Step 1

Pick up 3A beads and 1B bead. Go back through them all (diag. 1).

Step 2

Arrange your work so that it looks like diag. 2.

Step 3

Pick up 3A. Go around and up through the B bead (diag. 3).

Step 4

Pass through 2A beads (diag. 4).

Step 5

Pick up 1A, 1B and 1A bead (diag. 5).

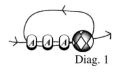

Diag. 1

Diag. 2

Diag. 3

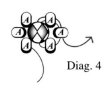

Diag. 4

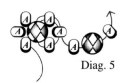

Diag. 5

Step 6

Pass down through the A bead you were coming out of (diag. 6).

Diag. 6

Step 7

Pass through the next A and B beads (diag. 7).

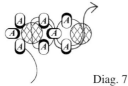

Diag. 7

Repeat from diags 3 to 7 for the length required, ending after diag. 4. When you have the required length, go back and embellish with A beads.

TIP: Work about a dozen crystals into a chain and then go on and embellish as below, returning later to add further length as required.

Step 8

Come through the centre A bead, then through the next A bead (diag. 8).

Start here

Diag. 8

Step 9

Pick up 5A beads (diag. 9).

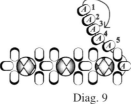

Diag. 9

Step 10

Pass down through the fourth bead from the needle end, to make a picot (diag. 10).

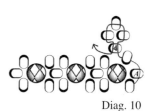

Diag. 10

Step 11

Pick up 1A bead, pass through the next A bead. Pass down through the central A bead of the group and the next A bead (diag. 11).

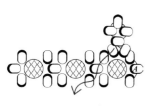

Diag. 11

Repeat from diags 9 to 11 all the way along alternate edges of your chain.

Step 12

Bring your thread through the next 2A beads as in diag. 12.

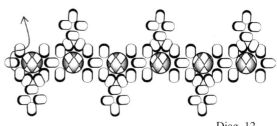

Diag. 12

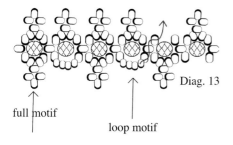

Diag. 13

full motif

loop motif

Diag. 13

Decide which side will be the top or neck edge. On this side you will work picots as before. On the underside there will be a plain loop of 3 or 4A beads (diag. 13).

The number of beads for the loop depends on the size of central bead that you use. Use only 3A beads if it looks better, but remember later on to adjust the number of beads that you go through when you work the half rosette around the 6mm beads in the next step.

Adding a beaded clasp at one end of the necklace

If you are adding this beaded catch then you will start with this instead of a stopper bead as shown in diag. 15. If you prefer though simply add a nice bought catch once you have finished.

Look at your work as it is in diag. 13. Either end will be like this. At one end you will add two full motifs for the clasp and at the other you will work a beaded loop.

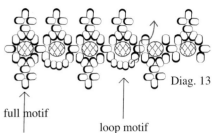

Diag. 13

full motif

loop motif

Step 1

For the clasp work two more full motifs like this: add 1A, 1B, 1A as in step 5 (diag. 13a).

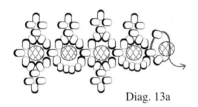

Diag. 13a

Step 2

Add 3A as in step 3 (diag. 13b).

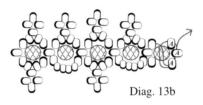

Diag. 13b

Step 3

Add 1A, 1C, 1A as in step 5 (diag. 13c).

Diag. 13c

Step 4

Add 3A as in step 3 (diag. 13d).

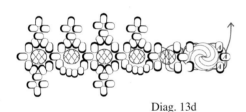

Diag. 13d

Step 5

Put picots on as before by working Steps 9, 10, 11 and 12 and turn (diag. 13e).

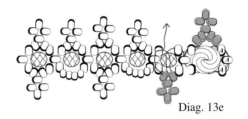

Diag. 13e

Add an extra bead to go around the larger C bead.

Step 6

Put picots on as before by working Steps 9, 10, 11 and 12 and turn (diag. 13f).

Diag. 13f

Now needle through to the loop motif as shown in diag. 15. You will not now need to have a new thread or stopper bead.

Make sure that your work is orientated in the correct way.

At the other end - when you have the length correct - make a beaded loop.

To fasten your necklace place the large and small full motifs through the loop. Make sure that the loop is not too large or the full motifs will fall through.

The Half Rosettes

Diag. 14

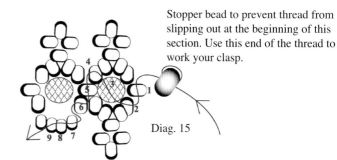

Stopper bead to prevent thread from slipping out at the beginning of this section. Use this end of the thread to work your clasp.

Diag. 15

Step 1

Start with your work looking like diag. 14

Start with a new thread and needle through beads 1 to 9 (diag. 15). If you changed the number in the loop on the underside in diag. 13 be careful how many beads you come through now. Stop and think! You need more than one bead to make a firm base for your rosette.

Step 2
Brick Stitch

Pick up 1C bead.
1. Go around back through the 2A beads of the loop.
2. Then pass around the bead.
Repeat this once.
You will have 2 strands of thread around your C bead (diags 16 and 17).
Adjust threads carefully and try to keep C central.

Diag. 16

Diag. 17

Step 3

Pick up 4A.
Pass needle under both threads around C.
Split beads into two columns of 2.
Pass needle up through the closest column of 2 beads (diags 18 and 19).

Diag. 18

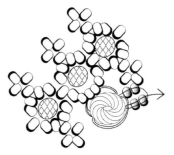

Diag. 19

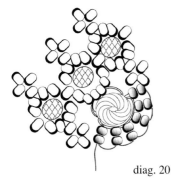

diag. 20

Step 4

Pick up 2A. Pass needle under both threads around C. Pass needle up through both of the beads. Repeat three more times creating 6 stacks of 2 beads in total. Pull stacks together so that no loose thread shows between the stacks (diag. 20)

Step 5
Herringbone Stitch

Turn your work to match diag. 21. Pick up 4A.

Go down through the next 2 bead stack and up the next stack.

Repeat twice more.

Now pass your needle down through the C bead (diag. 21).

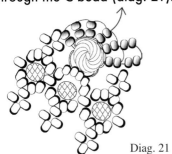

Diag. 21

Step 6

The diagram shows a large amount of thread, but you should pull your work tightly together to eliminate this as you work.

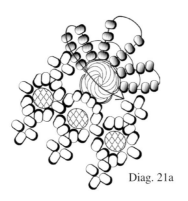

Diag. 21a

Step 7

Come up the first column of A beads (diag. 22).

Pull everything together fairly tightly.

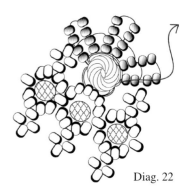

Diag. 22

Step 8

You now can see 3 stacks of 2 beads.

Pick up 2A beads. Go down through the next 2 beads in the first stack, and up through the top 2 beads of the next stack.

Repeat twice more.

Come back down the C bead (diags 23, 23a and 23b).

Pull together tightly, so no thread shows!

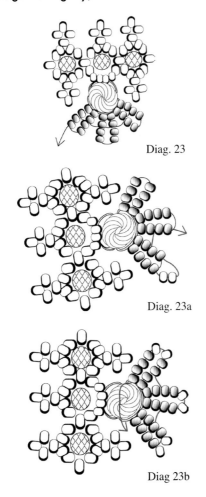

Diag. 23

Diag. 23a

Diag 23b

Step 9

Come up the first column of A beads.

Pick up 3A. Go down through the next 3 beads in the first stack and up through the top 3 beads of the next stack.

Repeat twice more.

Come back down the C bead (diags 24 and 24a).

Pull up tightly to eliminate loose thread.

Diag. 24

Diag. 24a

Step 10

Now the tricky bit - getting to the next loop! Logically you are following the previous thread path.

1. Back through your loop beads.

2. Diagonally up through the B bead.

3. Diagonally down through the ⚬ part of the ⚬

4. Diagonally up through the B bead.

5. Diagonally down through the ⚬ part of the ⚬

6. Come through your loop beads ready to start a new rosette (diag. 25).

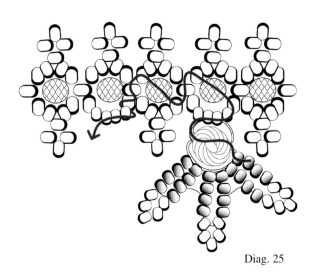

Diag. 25

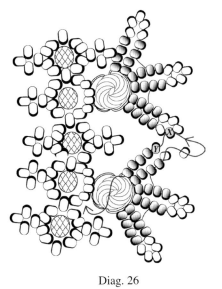

Diag. 26

Step 11

When you are in the correct place with your thread, start another half rosette (diag. 16). Work through from diags 16 to 23. Next you work the first two columns as you did in diag. 24, but for the last column you join this new half rosette to the previous one, like this:

The Join

1. Come up the third column. Pick up 1A. Go down the top bead of the first column on the previous half rosette, marked X.

2. Come back to this half rosette and go down the top bead of the last column, marked Y.

3. Continue down the column and through the C bead as before (diag. 26).

4. Go back to diag. 25 and work rosettes along your chain.

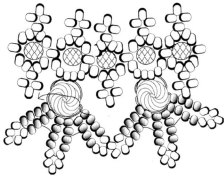

Step 12

Work both the Chain section and the Half Rosette section for the length required. Add a bought clasp, or bead a catch, and finish all ends away neatly.

Rosettes

Seed Bead size 11/0 ④ or Size 10/0 Hex ⬡
Oval Pressed Beads size 6mm or slightly larger ⬭
Delica Drop Beads ⬮ or you can use crystals

Steps 1 and 2

Prepare one wide arms length of thread. Go through and around one side of the B bead (diag. 1). Then go around the other side and come out as in diag. 2.

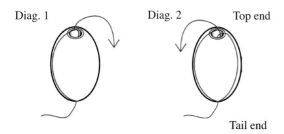

Step 3

Repeat Steps 1 and 2. Bring thread back out at the top end of B (diag. 3).
Turn the bead on its side (diag. 4).

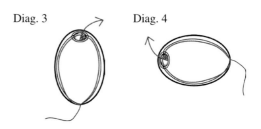

Step 4

Pick up 2A beads. Pass needle under both threads on one side of B. Bring needle up through second A bead (diag. 5).

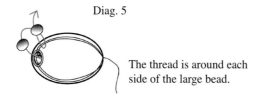

The thread is around each side of the large bead.

Step 5
Brick Stitch

Pick up 1A bead. Pass the needle under both threads on one side of B. Bring the needle up through this bead (diag. 6).

Step 6

Work step 5 around both sides of the B bead, then back around the other side. Number of beads each side should be the same. Try out odd and even numbers on each side, the total must be divisible by 2 (diags 7 and 8).

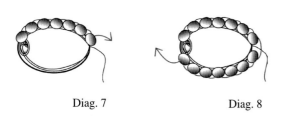

Step 7
Herringbone Stitch

Turn work around. Pick up 2A beads. Go down through the next bead, then up the next one.

Pick up 2A beads (diags 9 and 10).

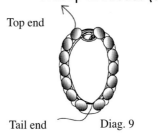

Step 8

Go down the next bead and up the next. Pick up 2A beads. Pull work together well at the tail end. Repeat step 8 all the way around the B bead (diags 11 and 12).

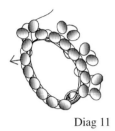

Diag 11

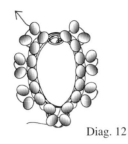

Diag. 12

Step 9

You can now see stacks of 2 beads all around your oval bead. Pick up 1A, 1C, 1A. Go down through the next bead in the first stack, and up through the first bead of the next stack. Pick up 1A, 1C, 1A (diags 13 and 14).

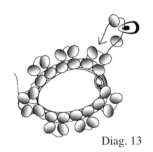

Diag. 13

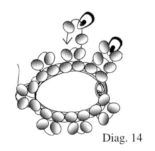

Diag. 14

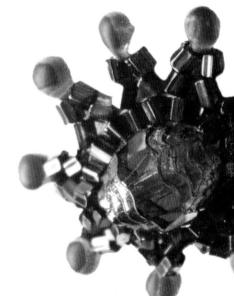

Step 10

Go down through the next bead in the stack, and up through the first bead of the next stack. Pick up 1A, 1C, 1A. Repeat all the way around (diag. 15).

Lastly!

Neaten all ends. You might want to add an extra bead at the top end or in between stacks. Make another rosette to match and attach earring or brooch findings to suit (diag. 16).

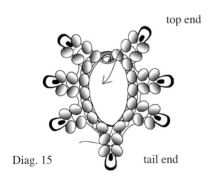

top end

Diag. 15   tail end

optional extra bead or beads

bead added between each stack

Diag. 16

Examples:

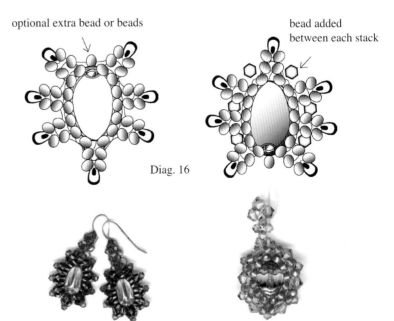

Treasure Trove

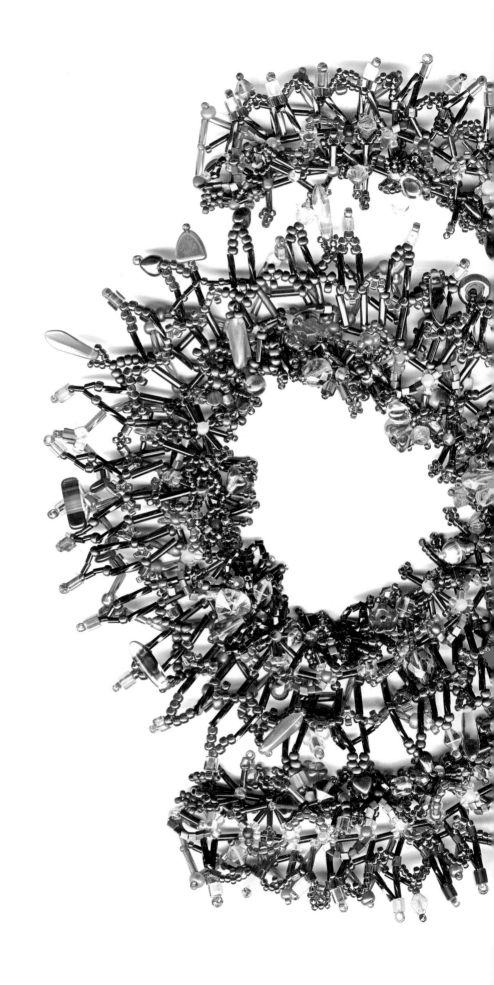

This necklace is built up in layers. Each layer can become the final necklace. A clasp can be added at any stage and the necklace worn as it is. Then, if you would like to, add another round at a later date when you have more time and inclination! You could work the rounds as they are written here to obtain a necklace like the original, or go from the foundation row, round 1 straight to rounds 5 and 6. I liked the foundation row so much that I made several in different colours before I went on to complete the whole necklace!

Notes on your choice of beads

Here is a rough list of the beads I have used. Try not to feel totally ovewhelmed! I have not stated any amounts. It is fun to use up odds and ends, moving from one colour to the next.

Read through the notes and diagrams and get out the treasures that you have in your collection. Put them together and then choose some seed beads of different sizes to go with them. As long as you have the beads listed for the foundation row and round 1, the rest will seem to follow.

I have also listed the beads as they are used in each round.

Colour - Think of a colour scheme that you would like to bead.

Have you an outfit you would like to wear this with?

What about trying out some colours you wouldn't usually use?

Look at your colour wheel. Hopefully this will give you some inspiration.

We are going for colour and texture, so don't forget to put some frosted and opaque beads into your collection.

Bead	Symbol	Code
Size 8/0 seed bead	◗	A
6mm bugle bead	▭	B
Size 15/0 seed bead	•	C
Delica drop bead	◖	D
Size 11/0 bead	◖	E
Size 6/0 seed bead	◗	F
Seed large square bead	▢	G
Shaped bead	◆	H
Donut	◯	J
Dagger	▽	K

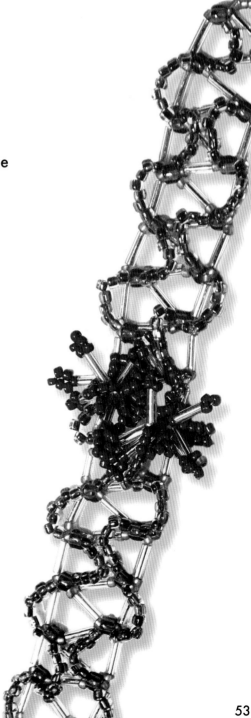

Choosing your beads continued...

Remember you don't have to choose all your beads before you start. The necklace can and will grow and change as you work. The only rounds that you should use exactly the same beads as I have are the foundation row and round 1. The first 2 rounds can end up being totally covered in other beads, so if you decide that you want to change colour it is possible to do that over the next few rounds.

Make sure that the bugle beads you use are good quality. Check your bugle beads, throw out any suspect ones, they will cut your thread all too easily.

Notes on thread and working technique

Use a D thickness thread, doubled and well waxed. The wax will not only keep the two threads under control but will also help you to obtain a tighter tension for your foundation row. Pull the thread through slowly and carefully as you work. If you find it impossible to work with a double thread go back to using a single thread, but you will need to go through the first layer again to re-inforce it.

Change to a single thread for the second layer onwards.

Always pull your thread through in the same direction that you pass through the bead. This will help you to maintain a tight tension and reduce the risk of cutting the thread on the bugle beads. If your thread does break do not panic, simply add another thread and knot in as usual.

Make sure that all the drop beads are facing the same way. Twist carefully!

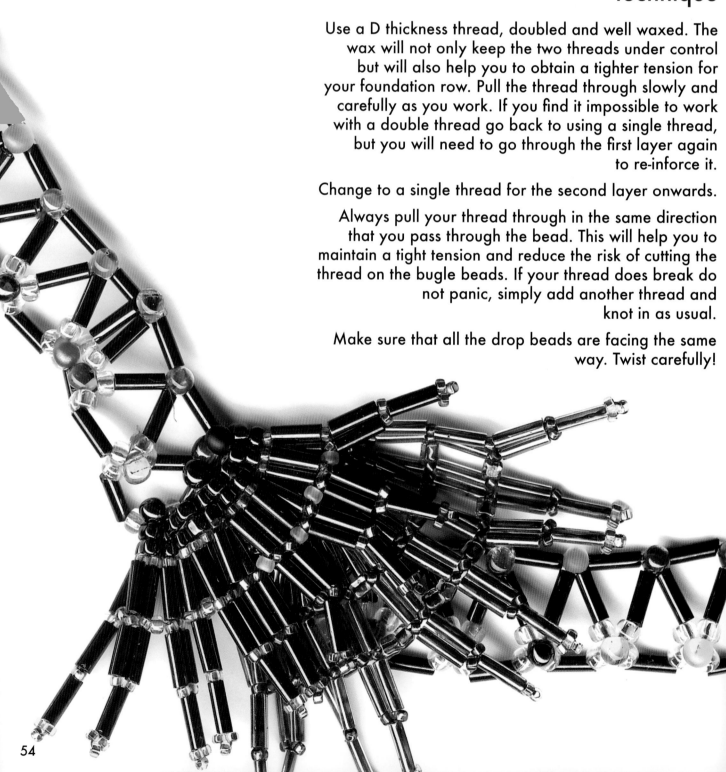

Treasure Trove

The original Treasure Trove Necklace.
All the rounds have been worked as written here in the book.

Treasure Trove – Fan Necklace
Work the foundation row, then add a clasp and cover this with herringbone fan motifs.

Treasure Trove – Mini Bracelet
Work the foundation row, followed by round 5 and use one motif from round 6.

Treasure Trove – Mini Necklace
Work the foundation row, followed by rounds 5 and 6.

So, let's start at the beginning with the foundation row. Try out different colours here, add a clasp and make a plain necklace.

Section 1 The Foundation Row

We start with a very pretty variation of the Chevron Chain. This does get rather covered up so don't worry if you change your mind about colour later or feel that you have made a mistake in your initial choice. Take your beads out of their containers and put them together on your cloth to check that you like the effect that they are creating. Now to start!

Materials

Size 8/0 seed bead	○	A
Bugle bead	▬	B
Size 15/0 seed bead	•	C
Delica Drop Bead	◊	D

Step 1 The start

Pick up 1D, 1B, 1A, 1D, 1A, 1B, 1A, 1D, 1A, 1B (diag. 1).

Bead 1

Diag. 1

Pass back up through bead marked 1 (a drop bead). See picture left and diag. 2.

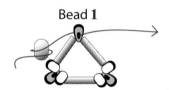

Bead 1

Diag. 2

Step 2 The repeat, part 1

Pick up 1C, 1B, 1C, 1D, 1B, 1A. Pass back down through bead marked 2 (a drop bead). See diag. 3 and picture below.

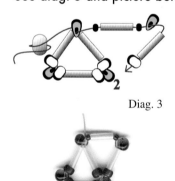

Diag. 3

Step 3 The repeat, part 2

Pick up 1A, 1B, 1A, 1D, 1A, 1B. Pass back up through bead marked 3 (a drop bead). See diags 4 and 4a and picture right.

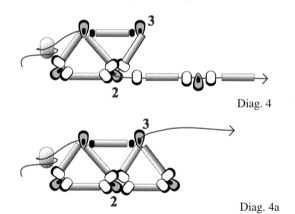

Diag. 4

Diag. 4a

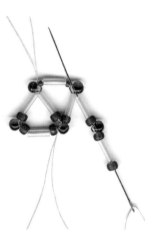

To continue...

Repeat steps 2 and 3 for length required.

Things to think about while you are beading:
1. How long do you want your necklace?
2. Do you want a central focal point?
3. Have you a special (large) bead you want to put into the necklace?
4. Do you want to have an opening or catch?

Experiment!

Further experiments for future necklaces and chains: try out different types, colours and numbers of beads in all sections of the chain.
What worked?
Why does the chain curve?

Before you start to bead this round it is a good idea to mark the centre point of the necklace with a small piece of contrasting thread. Also mark each side where the necklace sits on the collar bone. As you work you will graduate the size of your additions and embellishments, getting larger from the centre back round to the centre front and then reducing on the other side to match.

Section 2 - Round 1

On this round we set down some beads to bead onto and into. If you have large bugles that is good, or smaller ones can be built up by placing beads in between. These breaks also give us extra holes to come out of and use for more embellishment.

Please note very carefully:

Round 1 is worked over alternate groups of size 8/0 bead flowers as in these diagrams.

When working this as Round 3 all groups of bead flowers are worked. For slightly less texture work through the empty flowers only.

Work back along the foundation row like this:

Come out of an 8/0 bead as shown in the diagram below.

<table>
<tr><td>Bugle bead</td><td>▭</td><td>B</td></tr>
<tr><td>Size 11/0 seed bead</td><td>◊</td><td>E</td></tr>
<tr><td>Size 6/0 seed bead</td><td>◊</td><td>F</td></tr>
<tr><td>Large Square Bead</td><td>▫</td><td>G</td></tr>
</table>

Materials

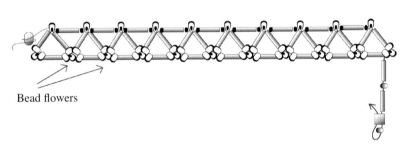

Bead flowers

Step 1

Pick up 1B, 1E, 1B, 1G, 1E.
Pass back up through bead G.
Pull up tightly.

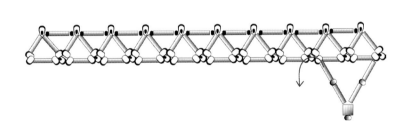

Step 2

Pick up 1B, 1E, 1B, miss one flower.
Pass back up through the first 8/0 bead of the flower then across and through the other 8/0 flower bead in the foundation row.
NB Do not pass through the drop bead.

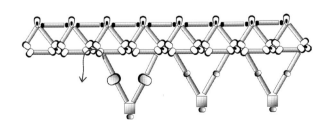

Step 3

Repeat step 2 a few times.
Now gradually get longer and larger.
Pick up a 6/0 bead in between bugles instead of an 11/0.

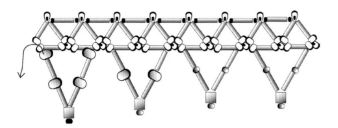

Step 4

Repeat Step 3 a few times.

Now gradually get longer and larger again.

Pick up a 6/0 bead after you come out of the top 8/0. At the same time put one in between the bugles as before.

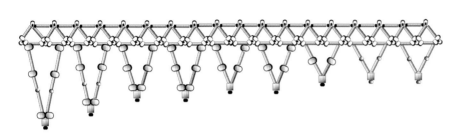

Step 5

Use more beads and more sections of bugles, or use larger beads and longer bugles.

Make a nice smooth graduation to the centre front of your necklace and back again, finishing at the centre back.

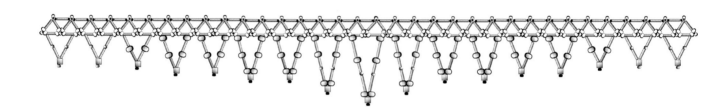

Section 3 Round 2

Now we start embellishing and playing! Stop and admire your necklace so far. Take a break and get ready to tackle the next round. You could stop now, add a clasp, wear it for a while and continue another day.

Materials

Bugle bead	▭	B
Size 11/0 seed bead	◯	E
Size 6/0 seed bead	◯	F
Large square bead	▢	G
Shaped bead	◆	H
Dagger	◇	K
Donut	◎	J

Now we are going to make these points stable by working in between them at areas A and B.

Make sure that your thread is coming out the same bead in the same direction as this diagram on the right. If you are right handed turn your work over to continue.

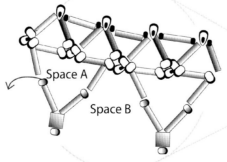

Space A

Space B

For enlargement see left

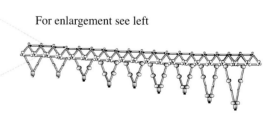

Step 1 Space A

In each space A work this sequence.

Pick up 1E, 1B, 1E.

Pass down through the opposite seed bead.

Space B

In each space B a variety of sequences can be worked.

Use your beads to gradually scale and shape your necklace. Also start to use some daggers, leaves and other interesting beads to shape and add interest.

Step 2

Pick up 1E, 1B, 2E, 1H, 1E. Pass around the last seed bead back through bead H and the next E bead.

Step 3

Pick up 1E, 1B, 2E, 1H, 1E.

Pass around the last seed bead back through bead H and the next E bead.

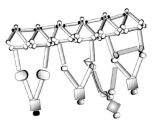

Here are several alternatives. Use whatever treasures you have in your trove.

Section 4 Rounds 3 and 4

Stop and admire your necklace again. Take a break. Decision time – do you want to go further with adding texture? If not you could skip Rounds 3 and 4 and go straight to Section 5 and bead Round 5 if you would like.

Once again, this can make a very pleasant necklace if beads are chosen carefully.

Round 3

Now, if you choose, put on another layer by working rounds 1 and 2 in a similar way again. When you repeat round 1 work into every group of bead flowers (size 8/0 beads) on the base of the chevron foundation round.

Do not use size 6/0 beads but use more size 8/0 beads, bugles, squares, leaves - whatever treasures you have.

Bugle bead	▬▬▬	B
Size 11/0 seed bead	⬭	E
Large square bead	▢	G
Shaped bead	◆	H
Dagger	◁▷	K
Donut	◎	J

Materials

Round 4

Infill in area B as before, but if you don't need too much more texture just add groups of beads size 11/0 and 8/0 or make a berry like this:

Pick up 4 beads.

Bring needle around and through the first 3 beads just picked up.

Pull together tightly to get a little berry.

This can also be done with extra beads each side of the berry.

Pick up 5 beads and make a berry. Pick up 1 bead.

Pick up 6 beads and make a berry. Pick up 2 beads.

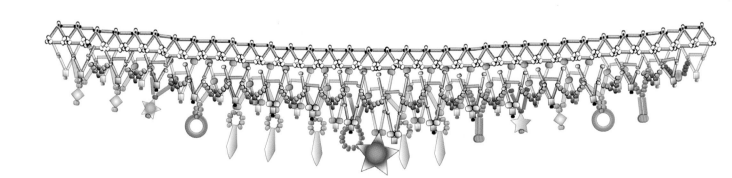

Section 5 Round 5

You will work through the bottom row of your chevron chain foundation row, where you have already worked the first few rows. This time use the drop beads (the centre of the flowers). Look at the picture below, this makes a very nice project without other embellishments.

Round 5

If you are finding the top of your necklace too boring and want more texture, start to embellish it now.

Come up through the centre drop bead.

Pick up around 9 beads - numbers depend on the size of beads chosen.

Go down through the next drop bead along.

Pick up around 9 beads - numbers depend on the size of beads chosen.

Go up through the next drop bead along.

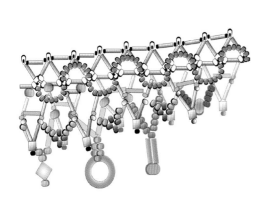 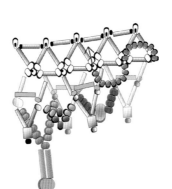 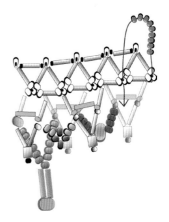

This picture shows Round 5 worked straight onto the foundation row. This too makes a very interesting necklace. Round 5 could also be worked into the top row of drop beads.

What else can be done with these loops?

Investigate using different sizes, colours and shapes of beads

If you have had enough beading you could stop after Round 5 - simply add a clasp and your necklace could look like this.

Section 6 Round 6

This could be the last round!

Bugle bead		B
Size 11/0 seed bead		E
And/or size 15/0 seed bead	●	C

Round 6

This round embellishes the top of the necklace. We will cover the chevron chain foundation row with more treasures and texture. You could even add crystals here too.

Bring your thread out of a drop bead

Pick up 1B and 5E. Go back through the B and the drop bead. Pull tightly. Repeat 3 or 4 times, until you like the result.

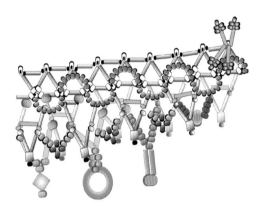

Alternatives to be used.
What else can you think of?

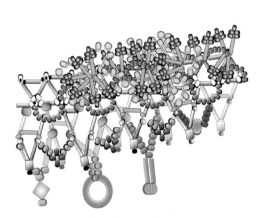

Move along to the next D bead. Do this by picking up about 7 or 8 E beads and go up or down through the next D bead.

What alternatives can you think of to move from drop bead to drop bead?

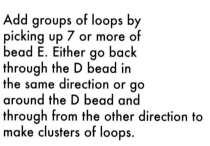

Add groups of loops by picking up 7 or more of bead E. Either go back through the D bead in the same direction or go around the D bead and through from the other direction to make clusters of loops.

Watch your colours – keep to maybe two colours.

Don't forget to vary size and type of bead.

Introduce some treasures, crystals and accent beads to keep the eye interested all the way around.

Make the texture heavier as you get towards the centre and lighter from your collarbone to the back of your neck. Too much texture will catch long hair in the beads.

Affix a nice solid fastener.

Wear with pride!

The version pictured left was made by working the foundation row and then Rounds 5 and 6 only.

Herringbone Fan

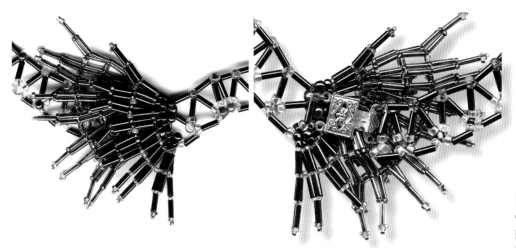

Materials

Size 10/0 triangle bead
(or a size 8/0)
6mm bugle bead
Size 15/0 seed bead

Ladder Stitch Start - This is
a useful start to many bead
projects. For this one, use the
size 10/0 triangle beads.

Use this to cover a clasp and add decoration to a simple necklace

Step 1

Pick up 4 beads
Go around and
back through all
beads (diag. 1).

Diag. 1

Step 2

Arrange beads
in 2 stacks of 2
beads (diag. 2).

Diag. 2

Step 3

Pick up 2 beads
Go back through
the adjacent
stack of 2 beads
(diag. 3).

Diag. 3

Step 4

Now pass your
needle up the
stack of 2 beads
just picked up
(diag. 4).

Diag. 4

Step 5

Pick up 2 beads
Go back through
the adjacent
stack of 2 beads
(diag. 5).

Diag. 5

Step 6

Now pass your
needle down the
stack of 2 beads
just picked up
(diag. 6).

Diag. 6

Row 1

Pick up 1 seed bead, 1 bugle, 2
seed beads, 1 bugle.

Go back down through bead 10
and 9. Come back up the next 2
beads (diags 7 and 8).

Repeat all along the foundation row.
To turn your work simply tie a knot
and come back up the beads you
are exiting from so that your thread
comes out of the edge group of
beads (diag. 9).

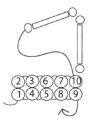

Diag. 7

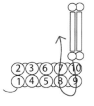

Diag. 8

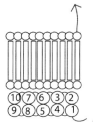

Diag. 9

Row 2

*Pick up 1 bugle, 2 seed beads, 1 bugle.

Go back down through the second part of the first stack and up the first part of the second stack* (diag. 11).

Repeat from * to * on top of each stack (5 stacks).

Turn work and bring thread out of the first side of the first stack (diag. 12).

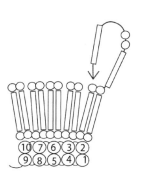
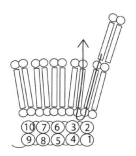
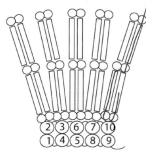

Diag. 11

Diag. 12

Row 4

*Pick up 1 bugle, 3 seed beads.

Go back down through the bugle and then the second part of the first stack (diag. 13).

Pick one seed bead and pass up the first part of the second stack* (diag. 14).

Repeat from * to * on top of each stack (5 stacks).

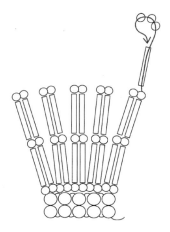
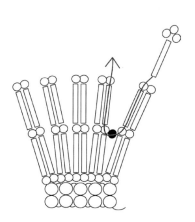

Diag. 13

Diag. 14

Fasten all ends off neatly all (diag. 15).

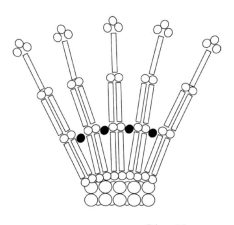

Diag. 15

Make one or two to cover a clasp.

Make several and turn them into a circular pendant.

Try making them in a circle.

How many will you need to start with in the foundation row?

Experiment!

Experiment with another row of bugle beads, different types, colours and numbers of beads.